A COLLECTION OF ORIGINAL POETRY

From Girl to Grown Woman

RELATIONSHIPS & ROMANCE

Gerre' Myrte'

COLLEGE BOY
PUBLISHING
"We Breed Bestsellers"

DALLAS, TX, USA

From Girl to Grown Woman
Relationships & Romance

Published by College Boy Publishing
ISBN: 978-1-944110-55-0
Printed in the United States of America

Without limiting the rights under copyright reserved above, no part of this publication may be reproduced, stored in, or introduced into a retrieval system, or transmitted, in any form, or by any means, electronic, mechanical, photocopying, recording, or otherwise), without prior written permission of both the copyright owner and the above publisher of thie book.

PUBLISHER'S NOTE
The scanning, uploading, and distribution of this book via the Internet or via any other means without the permission of the publisher is illegal and punishable by law. Please purchase only authorized electronic and physical editions, and do not participate in or encourage electronic piracy of copyrighted materials. Your support of the author's rights is appreciated.

To order copies of this book or to book a training for your organization, please contact Family Rise Together via phone at +1-972-591-3739 or the website **CollegeBoyPublishing.com** for more info.

Copyright 2025. Gerre' Myrte. All rights reserved.

Introduction from the Author

My poetry writing started from my days of high school. I had words in my head and they needed to come out, so I put them on paper. I love the way words can rhyme, and I love the way words are used to express feelings. Sometimes when you can't say what you want to say verbally, write it out and let the words flow. Words are a beautiful expression, and poetry is the key to bringing it in to form.

My favorite poet is Langston Hughes. He leaves the reader wondering is there more to come.
I want readers to wonder that about my poetry.

I'm a mother to 5 children and two grandchildren. I'm the oldest sister of three. I'm the wife to an amazing husband, Thomas. I'm the daughter of two school teachers. I'm happy that I get to share my expressions and heart with the world. I love poetry and I love how it makes me feel.

Gerre' Myrte'

Table of Contents

Title	Page
Under The Covers	1
Away	2
I am	3
A Regret for Loving You	4
Way back When	5
Miss Someone	6
Never Would've Made It	7
Happy Birthday	8
You and Me	9
Breathe	10
Never	11
Just Don't Know How Much	12
Orange Juice	13
I Love the Way	14
Daddy Dearest	15
For P.j.j	16
It's You	17
Lonely Again	18
No You Without Me	19
Future	20
From Breakup to Not Making Up	21
Michael's Poem	22
Friendship	23
My First Poem	24
Never Meant to Be	25
Passionate	26
Together	27
Pillows	28

Table of Contents

Title   **Page**

Title	Page
Waiting	29
The Grove	30
Quiet Storm	31
Loneliness	32
Fullers	33
Honey Gone	34
See The Real You and Me	35
Cherished	26
Gold	27
Child Please	38
Love	39
Only You	40
However	41
My Worth	42
Proverb Woman	43
Touch of Me	44
Like You Say You Do	45
Remembering the Memories	46
A Love Like Ours	47
Leaving You	48
Doing Things Together	49
First Sight	50
Coochie Drop	51
August Mine	52
August Mine (Cont.)	53
Grind	54
I Know You Love When	55

From Girl to Grown Woman

RELATIONSHIPS & ROMANCE

Under The Covers

Silently, your moans turn to a cry
From the beautiful lovemaking
From the sexing between my thighs
When you're trying to be one with me
And every little pump you give
Takes me to a higher place upon which we want to live

Tears are falling, and I see it in your eyes
The depth of which you love me
And just how much your heart cries

Slowly grinding, slowly pushing, to the point of no return
Your sex is freakin' awesome, and every day I yearn
Milk chocolate, laced with the "OMG," yes!!!!!
Can't wait to see you everyday, cause your &#$* is so Blessed
Here we go again, another time, another date
Just by the strokes you give, I know you are my mate
Pound for pound, every time you are up to mount
I anxiously await just what is coming out

Your love is sweeter than candy, richer than gold
You had me from day one; my heart, you do hold
Lay back, close your eyes, and I am right there
Can you smell me? Can't you taste me in the air?

Touch me, rub me, please me while I'm on top
You are my everything; you are the cream of the crop.

09/17/2014 Gerre' Mua

Away

From the inside out to the outside in
I tried to sway you over, but I couldn't win
We laughed and kissed under the moonlight
Something in your heart said it wasn't right
I love the way you look, from your head to your toes
I've told you I love you, and you said, "I know."
The touch of your hand is all too much
I wiggle and squirm from a simple touch
Underneath, I wanna reach out and grab you
I got to keep my composure; It's not easy to do

I just wanna say I'll always be here
I'll always keep you close and always keep you near
Just close your eyes and think of me
I'm very far away, but not too far to see
I'll close my eyes and think of you
And pray one day, our love will be true.

02/20/1994 Gerre' Flemons

I Am

Without you, I am nothing
Without you, I am blue
Without you, I am empty
And I don't know what to do.

Without you, life is endless
Without you, I can't go on
Without you, I cry all night
Until the break of dawn.

Without you, I don't crack a smile
Without you, I don't care
Without you, I just hold my head down
Because love is something I used to share.

Without you, I don't eat, or I don't sleep
Without you, I toss and turn
Without you, I just gaze at the stars
And every day, I yearn.

Gerre' Flemons - 12/10/1992

A Regret for Loving You

Why do my feelings for you come and go?
Sometimes I just want to let you know
How I feel when I see ya'll together
I used to think you and I would be together forever
A love like the one I thought the both of us had
It brings a person joy, you know, makes them glad
Everyone kept saying you were not the one for me
In my mind, I kept thinking, How can that be?

I said, "He's very special, and we will never break up."
Because I feel the love between us when he gives a touch.
Momma always said, "Love doesn't last forever.
So baby, be careful, and baby, be clever.
Don't let a man misuse or abuse you."
I'm happy she told me, so next time I'll know what to do.
I'm slowly but surely getting over the way I feel.
I still love you. I've got to be for real
If that was love, I want to be alone.
Now my heart's colder than ice and hard as stone
I don't know if I'll ever love again,
Or love them as much as I loved you then.

Gerre' Flemons -10/09/1992

Way Back When

Seems like only yesterday we talked briefly face to face.
I smiled, you smiled, and my heart began to race.
The gleam in your light brown eyes touched my inner soul.
I needed you in my life to really make me whole.
Figured out why I can love you so very much
The fact remains that when I feel your tender touch

My legs tremble, my eyes are glazed, and I'm in awe
Because you're the Man,
you came over, you conquered, and you saw
Whether it was yesterday, today, or tomorrow,
my dear sweetest love
You are surely a gift from the Man up above.

Gerre' Flemons - 10/07/1996

Miss Someone

You never really know how much you miss someone
Until they are gone, and nothing can be done
Then you'll want that person to share your love again
So he'll surprise you with a gift every now and then
I had a special person that I loved very much
But I let him get away, and now I can't feel his touch
Of the warmth, we used to share when the night was very young
I got hurt with love, and, boy, that really stung
I kinda hate to think of the love we used to share
We were always playing and laughing without any care
Then one day, I realized that he was the one
You never really know how much you miss someone.

Gerre' Flemons - 08/29/1992

Never Would've Made It

The laugh, the cries
The sorrows, the lies
I trusted you; I believed in you
I moved away from my home for you
I changed, you changed
Our lives will never be the same
My heart is broken; I don't think you love me anymore
Sorry I cannot be the woman that you adore
The lies you gave about a child
Had me going that extra mile
Oh, the cries you say, "Stop it right now!"
My emotions are flowing, and I don't know how...
I'm not happy; you're not happy; I can see it in your eyes
Even when I touch you in places, I don't get a reaction
The saying is: "Set it free; if it comes back to you, it is yours."

Unknown Date Gerre' Mua

Happy Birthday

For Stacy Bishop, My Love

Have a very nice birthday
And many more to come
Please don't drink too much
Party all night long
You deserve the very best

By your side is where I'll be
If not forever, till you're tired of me
Remember, I love you
This day you're one year younger
Happy birthday my big head brother
Don't be down and out; stay sweet
And always remember
You're thought of and loved dearly!!

05/26/1996 Gerre' Flemons

You and Me

Your smile I see each day I wake will light up any room
It shines so bright at night that there's no need for any moon
Touch me, feel me, caress me, lay me down to rest
Make sweet, compassionate love to me; I have to have the best
Treasure the goodness that I have deep down in my soul
Not to have you in my life would mean I wasn't whole
Touch me, feel me, caress me, lay me down to rest
Stroke her, tease her, please her, now… not next
Smile with those beautiful brown eyes and set my body on fire
Show me that I am your one and only desire
Open my center and fill it to the top, don't forget the brim
Listen to the ooh ahh sound I make when you put me in a whim
With the last push of your ecstasy,
Show me this is where we should be
To keep the torch burning and the love flowing through
So when we make love next time… it's you and me, you and me.

11/09/2000 Gerre' Flemons

Breathe

I breathe you in, and I can't get enough
Of the fragrance; people call that "good stuff"
I love you deep like a flesh wound on my cheek
Your love is so demanding; I often get too weak
I kiss the warmth of your sweet, tantalizing lips
As you work inside of my big pulsating hips
Deeper you are flowing, faster you are going
Up and down, and the faces you are showing
Love me completely; we are both aching
As we hit our joint from the pleasure of lovemaking
After all is said and surely done
Lie there and know that we are one
Breathe me like I breathed you
And know that after this…comes round 2.

10/16/2002 Gerre' Mua

Never

Never imagined my heart
Torn from grief or broken in half
Never imagined the emptiness I feel
Knowing I'll never hear your laugh
Never imagined how walking without your hand in mine
Could lead to total disaster of words that are so unkind
Never knew I was in a relationship of a web of pure lies
Never knew all along my efforts were only short tries
Never knew when I ached on the outside in
I was never going to be the one that would win
Never had the chance to really show you I hold your heart
Never had an opportunity to show you I was smart
Never had kind words cross your lips for me
All we ever seem to do is live in misery
So if I don't hold your heart and your soul
Please let me go so I may complete me as a whole.

10/10/2009 Gerre' Flemons

Just Don't Know How Much

Skin, the color of raven
Lips soft to the touch
I wanna love you down
Just don't know how much
The smile you give is bright
Like no other one I know
Your body of perfect build
Eyes all aglow

Skin, the color of raven
Lips soft to the touch
I wanna love you down
Just don't know how much
When you touch me softly
My body goes all numb
I'm still very young
Please don't think I'm dumb

Skin, the color of raven
Lips soft to the touch
I'm gonna love you down
Now I know how much.

11/20/1998 Gerre' Flemons

Orange Juice

Ask yourself, "What do I do for you"?
Ask yourself, "What makes the sky blue?
What about where goosebumps start
And the real shape of your lover's heart
Sample the sweetest nectar, and you've tasted me
Lick my fingers, my navel, until you hear me weep
Grasp my hips and touch my lips
It's like orange juice on the last few sips
Meaning, "Damn," it's almost gone
I wish I had some more
Of that sweet ass orange juice
Does the neighbor have some next door?
Can't get enough of that juicy taste
Don't let a drop miss your lips or waste
Cause, "Damn," what happened to you?
Is the sky blue?
What was it about goosebumps?
And what exactly is the reason?
For all this sweetness for every season
You said something about a navel and hips
Come here and let me get that off your lips
Oh, sweet thang!!!!!
Thanks for my sensual love swang!!!!!

I Love The Way

I love the way you watch me
I feel your eyes on me, and a smile
I know that it's still early
But I've wanted this for a while
The way you start to love me
The way you just seem to care
The way that you kiss my lips
Open up your heart to share
Don't be afraid of my love
Don't be afraid of my heart
Don't be afraid to trust me
Stop second-guessing our new start
Love!
Love!!
Love!!!
That's what I need from you
There is no pressure dear
Everything in my mind is clear
Free from doubt
Free from despair
Free from hurt
Free from dare.

Daddy Dearest

I'm standing in the kitchen with what we've made
A beautiful son that carries your last name
Somehow I thought our lives would be a fairy tale
Instead, I'm holding back tears and waiting for your mail
A phone call or a text, just to let our little one know
That you care or think of him or want to watch him grow
None of it happens, but he longs to have your embrace
To be in your presence, to have you put kisses on his face
I'm raising him to be a man and do the exact opposite of you
He has a heart that's pure as gold and a smile just like you do
You're walking around here like you have done something
When reality is, you ain't done nothing
Bragging about how you raised "my" son
Head held high like you have truly won
See, "my" son has a dad that put in work when he could
"Our" son wishes he had that, you know that, and should
One day when he's old enough to understand
Why you left him, and you weren't the man
That would help him stand up and be a grown man
You're off doing other things; guess you had different plans
I play catch with him; I'm at any sports event
I'm the type of parent that always has time spent
Whether tired or not, whether happy or sad
When our little one calls out, I've got to get glad
Thanks for nothing, my boy; I hope never to see you again
And I will definitely raise "our" son to be a better man.

05/01/2016 Gerre' Mua

For P.J.J.

There is opportunity between you and me
There are words to be said, don't you see
Since you've re-entered my life, I have you now
When I looked at you, your eyes said, "Wow!"
My heart was pumping with an abnormal beat
My heart shall be yours once the two of ours meet
Electrifying, captivating, this feeling is real
Having you in my life, now there is a deal
I'm loving you with every beat of my heart
Hope the feeling is mutual, so there is a start
For our love to grow, to be all that it can
For me to be your woman and you to be my man
I need to feel your warm embrace
I need to put kisses upon your face
How do you feel? Is your heart in this race?
Is the feeling the same? Can I see it on your face?
When I caress, does your body turn to a sweat?
Like the first day, I saw you, the first day we met
Pleasure is what I want you to feel
My heart for you to hold, and it's very real
Deeper than any love that you've ever been in
I want you to understand all I do is win
So take my heart, and please keep it safe
And I will do the same, keep yours in the place
Next to my love and next to the space
Where love stays, and God has His grace.

07/22/2011 Gerre' Mua

It's You

How did we end up kickin' it again
With you having a woman and me having a man
Seems like yesterday we were lovers and friends
That's gone now; it has come to an end
You said you're thinking of me sometimes
Probably when you imagine my juicy behind
The hug was off the chain; I have to say
The gentleness and warmth, why'd you bring it my way
Now you have a woman thinking to herself and things
What's the next step, and what this all brings
You say honesty all the way with me
I say let's take it slow, and let's just see
If this is the connection I've waited so long for
Or do you have to see my face wanting more
Crazy about you; always have been; always will be
Loving your light brown skin comes so natural to me
Thought I was ready to venture out on my own
Cause we are friends forever, and that's well known
For now, I think I'lll be so true to mine
But I'll be there always for you until the end of time.

Lonely Again

Lonely again is where I am
Lonely again is where I'll be
Lonely again is where I stand
I can't find anyone who matches me
Lonely again, lying on my bed
Lonely again, gazing at the moon
Lonely again, I cry sometimes
I have to find me someone soon
Lonely again, I thank God above
Lonely again, I breathe today
Lonely again, tomorrow's coming
While putting my hands together as I pray.
12/02/1995 Gerre' Flemons

No You Without Me

There is no me without you
You make my gray skies blue
Your touch each and every time
Has got me going out of my mind
Wouldn't do anything to hurt your heart
I told you all this from the start
You really always brighten my day
Kissing me, loving me, in every single way
You got my heart and all of me
You got my hand, don't you see
Our love is to last forever, my dear
You are the man I want from year to year
We match each other and are meant to be
There is no you without me.

Future

I chose you from the crowd on that cool Summer's day
I watched you closely, and you took my breath away
The feeling I had made me shiver quite a lot
The sensation deep within had me steaming hot
I really like how you made me feel
I imagined it, and it came real
I am every woman; my heart is of pure gold
I think I love you and the future we will hold.

11/24/1993 Gerre' Flemons

From BreakUp
to
Not Making Up

I rolled over to apologize and rolled over into your spot
Sleeping without you is so cold that I almost forgot
You had to go on another business trip again
Not actually realizing we weren't even friends
Because I said mean things and so you said some too
Breaking up is especially hard for me to do
I love you and I can't take back the horrible past
You are the only man for me, the very last
Dedication is what I promised when I said, "I DO" that day
To love, honor, and cherish me, is what I heard you say
What happened to the little things or the cute little smiles
My heart yearns for that which I haven't seen in awhile
Not making up and going our separate ways
Is like skipping a breath each and every day
Remembering is what makes life worth living
Accepting little gifts, but most of all giving
We went from breaking up to not making up
And that isn't the way it should be
We should honor everything in our vows and hopefully
I will still love you and you will still love me.

03/05/2005 Gerre' Mua

Michael's Poem

Looking at you every day of my life
Wishing one day I'd be your wife
Our future will be very full and bright
We'll make love under the moonlight
I'm a joy for any black man
Listen to me as I take your hand
I'll lead you to places we've never been
Why? You ask. Cause we are best friends
Guide you all over the deep blue seas
To learn languages such as French or Japanese
We'll walk the ocean side by side
Caress each other from time to time
When you are tired, I'll lay you down to rest
And I'll thank God for sending me the very best
Sweet dreams, my love, rest your eyes now
Think joyful things as I brush your eyebrow
For tomorrow I'll wake you, and another day will begin
And like yesterday, today, we will still be best friends.

02/01/1996 Gerre' Flemons

Friendship

Friendship is a simple word that we should all express
If a friend is down and feeling blue, just give a gentle caress
We are too far apart to show how we are feeling
We just got over broken hearts, but we are slowly healing
Now we've found each other to help us see it through
And now I'm especially happy that I have found you
It's only been a little while since we've known each other
I only hope our friendship could last a lot further.

03/30/1992 Gerre' Flemons

My First Poem

Like a meadow in the night
Like the sky so full of light
What is that sound we hear
Away so far, so clear and near
It is the sound of sweet kisses
Birds chirping and snake hisses
We found honesty and trust
No more shall we have to lust
Like a bird flying high
I've got to say goodbye.

09/26/1990 Gerre' Flemons

Never Meant to Be

We had a love just the other day
But you saw someone else and turned away
I was so sure our love would last
You packed your bags, and you left fast
I didn't think it would last very long
Now I see that I wasn't so wrong
I loved you, and you loved me
I guess that it was never meant to be.

02/18/1991 Gerre' Flemons

Passionate

We have a passionate love that has to be met
When I called you over, I didn't expect you to sit
Down and talk to me; I thought you'd stand
You sat down, looked at me, and took my hand
That was a surprise, I do admit
But yet and still, it wasn't a regret.

02/18/1991 Gerre' Flemons

Together

One kiss on the neck and I didn't know what to do
Kiss you back or say I truly love you
I did neither of the two; I just stood there in awe
I can't imagine what people said or what they saw
I wanted to hold you as bad as you wanted to hold me
With little time and no place to go, how could that be
Eventually, we both had to say our goodbyes
When I drove off, tears started rolling out my eyes
The time we spent together I will cherish forever
And hope one day we'll be together.

09/30/1992 Gerre' Flemons

Pillow

I rolled onto your pillow, and what did I find
You were not there, and I nearly lost my freakin' mind
It's been agony day after day of you not being here
I really have to think, and my mind is not so clear
Our misfortune and time apart, was it a sign?
Do we belong together? Are you my one and only find?
The sheets are slightly scented; I can smell your scent
I feel your touch; you have the arch, my back bent
Stroking me, loving me, filling me with creme
I suddenly awake; was this all just a dream
Your pillow is wet, and so are my thighs
I had it between my legs, wishing it was a dick rise
Phenomenal lover that I know that you are
I have you in my mind; you're my shooting star

12/23/2015 Written by Gerre' Mua

Waiting

Anticipation of what our first time will be like
My "P" thang twitching from the thought of "D"elight
Pythons gonna grip her and out I will scream
From the passionate lovemaking and all of this creme
The hugs, the touches, your hands all over my breast
I've waited a long time to feel those arms and that chest
I'm on top, and I'm riding for my life
Trying to figure out if I wanna be your wife
The heart wants what the heart wants, is what I'm told
People should go by that, to have and to hold
Soul mates, love mates
Switching gears in these sheets
I'm about to climax; this loves making me weak
We are one right now; I know your every move
I'm trying to make you wife me; I have something to prove
Flip me over on my side, go deeper with that thang
I feel every stroke, and you won't hear me complain
I'm holding "it" cause I want you to cum
Want the pleasure for both of us to get sum
Now put me on my stomach, slight arch in my back
The odds are against you; the odds are stacked
Open up them cheeks, slide in and touch
That sweet spot that I know you'll love so much
I'm a beast on my stomach, bring'em down every time
Cause when you're in the back, I gets down with mine
I'm there, hit that spot again; I feel it about to erupt
I feel you jerking; that "P" thang made you bust
I love you, lover, that was fit for a queen
That's what makes me cum back, if you know what I mean.

05/20/2016 Written by Gerre' Flemons

The Grove

Eyes closed, heart beating rapidly with every breath that I breathe
Breast rising, then falling, and your hand reaches my cleave
I'm antsy because I'm ready for the world, ready for some action
You and I know that I'm about to cum into some real satisfaction
You taste every inch of my body
I know you, and you know me
You are driving me crazy from the subtle touch of your tongue,
ECSTASY!!!!!
Your favorite spot is the "grove"
You lounge there a minute, then I explode
Lover, you don't know this, but I got a "Jones" for your love
I yearn for your touch, and you fit my body like a glove
This is what I've been dreaming of, and I'm wet as can be
Sitting here thinking about us, and you cumming inside me
That thick ass juicy dick pushing inside my spot
I'm screaming your name, and I don't want you to stop
The pressure is rising, and we about to climax
BAM! BOOM! There we go on our backs
Thanks are in order because you felt so good to me
I can't believe now that I have been set free.
Especially For You!!!!!

12/14/2015 Gerre' Mua

Quiet Storm

Listen to the wind, soft and light
Here comes a storm in the quiet night
The heaven above and the land below
Listen, listen to how the light wind blows
I smell the storm coming very soon
Standing by my window, gazing at the moon
Now I'll lay my head down to rest
And place my hands upon my chest
Close my eyes and get prepared and warm
For a dark and smooth, quiet storm.

09/19/1995 Gerre' Flemons

Lonliness

There's a feeling I can't touch because it's hidden deep within
A lust of excitement I barely feel caresses my dark skin
I long to have this emotion barred from the deep
So I won't die with the pain or, in the morning weep
As I sit and listen for the pain to come and answer me
I have to know one thing, "will it let me be?"
The pain that I am speaking of is exactly what you guessed
It is the one some people say is the cause named loneliness
I hate to feel this thing that they call loneliness
I have to release some anger and get it off my chest
I'll yell, scream, cry, or just sit very still
Until I figure out what a scholar never will
Why loneliness is steady just sweeping across the land
At a very high speed with just the wave of my hand
When I get calm and half asleep, I'll listen for some rain
In hopes of waking in the morning and hope it's not the same.

03/08/1994 Gerre' Flemons

Fuller

I've known you for just a little while
And already I'm beginning to like your style
You are sweet, cute, and very nice
When you talk, it's sweeter than spice
What we could have will be very special and sweet
A love like the one we will have will be hard to beat
Derian, the things you say
Brighten up my every day
If we start a relationship real soon
We will have fun kissing under the moon
Life is short; we both know
Don't ever leave, don't ever go.

09/13/1992 Gerre' Flemons

Honey Gone

You really don't know how I feel about you
By the way you talk, smile, and the things you do
I really care for you more than you know
When we are together, we both had that glow
It was hard to break us apart
Now you're gone, let's make a new start
I never realized how much you really meant to me
Until you were gone and I was too blind to see
I can't eat or sleep; I toss and turn on my pillow at night
Thinking about the way you used to hold me tight
I'm always thinking of you, day in and day out
The way you used to touch me made me wanna shout
I won't ever forget the things we used to do together
My love for you never left; it'll stay here forever.

1992 Gerre' Flemons

See the Real You and Me

Baby, I'm ready to share my whole life with you
Set and cuddle while we're gazing into the blue
Ecstasy every day of your whole life long
Choosing happiness with me is not all wrong
Closer and closer each day we should get
Instead of acting like we've just met
I'm not the plague; I come real with mine
Like putting smiles on your face and watching them shine
Peace be unto you, while I'm away, my love
I see you as my Angel, my sweet turtle dove
So on my high pedestal. there's only one spot
You lose now, and there's not another shot
Delicate as a rose petal dropped at a king's feet
I am the one, and that's very hard to beat
"(Picture me rollin')" far away with no looking back
Then you wonder why you're 23 and having a heart attack
Loves too much for you to grip upon, sweetheart
End it now, and you're almost back at the start
Together is how I always pictured the two of us
Riding together on that Greyhound bus
Relaxing, sharing each breath with each other
Not having a care for the next black brother
A wool's pulled down over our eyes
Tomorrow's a new day, a bigger sunrise
Watch it all go up in gigantic red flames
This is reality, my love; no time for any more games

10/09/1996 Gerre' Flemons

Cherished

Excuse me, Mr. Tall, dark and handsome, that's what I'm looking for
In you, Mr. Man, I found a new world to explore
Does it ever bother me when I see you someplace else
Wining, dining, caressing, loving, and spending our wealth
Of course, but our love runs deep as the oceans and seas
I'm gonna trust you and pray on my cute little knees
A good thing comes around only in one lifetime
You've picked yourself a doozy,
Something special, something genuine
Let it slip away, and life for you is incomplete
Remember this one thing, my dear, I'm very unique
Close your eyes, make me yours, and you'll be happy for eternity
Put me off, and you'll need that stable security
Love me and leave me, and tomorrow I may perish
And in your heart, you'd hold memories you'd wished you cherished.

10/08/1996 Gerre' Flemons

Gold

Eyes of a real light brown
Skin soft as gold
Touch warm as the sun
My heart, you might hold
I can tell you one thing
I am really glad we met
Now I can have a new friend
And there's no regret
You can wine and dine me
Take me out for a night stroll
Kiss me on the cheek
My heart, you might hold
Tell your friends about me
I am very smart,
Nice, funny, and cute
That's really hard to beat
You can keep me forever
Although I might get old
I only will get better
My heart, you will hold.

10/21/1995 Gerre' Flemons

Child Please

I have let you use me from the jump
I smile real big but stay in the dump
My heart thumps crazy when I see your smiling face
In the back of my mind, I yearn to feel your warm embrace
Your macho image won't last for very long
I'll weaken you; then you won't be strong
By "weaken," I mean to make you less proud to abuse me
I only want to love you, for you to love me, baby, can't you see
Together is where we belong throughout life
I want to show you I can be your wife
Companions are fine except when searching for a mate
I'd have to search the world over, and that I would hate.

03/12/1995 Gerre' Flemons

Love

Love in any language means the same, the whole world through
Love to me means caring, sharing, and loving only you
Love means doing for one another no matter what the task
Love means just doing it before the other asks
Love is a wonderful feeling, deep within our soul
Love will make you happy and sad until you grow old
I've been hurt severely by this thing called love
I look for help high, in the Heavens up above
No answer seems to come when I want it to
So sit and wonder just what can I really do
Love in any language means the same, the whole world through
I just thought I'd tell ya; I wanna give it to you.

06/03/1995 Gerre' Flemons

Only You

Each day my heart pumps fast from visions of you
As you lay beside me in the sweet morning dew
Our naked bodies wrapped together so tight
For all eternity, for the rest of our lives
Only you are for me, and I for you
What in the world is there left to do
We've been to the moon and back again
Only you had the courage to be my best friend
You've given me the world and kept me smiling
Wiped away my tears when I was crying
No one could ever do the things you do
That's why it's you and only you.

08/18/1995 Gerre' Flemons

However

Pain grows, and it is easily covering my chest
The beat of your heart is pounding on my chest
As we lay as one and I can hardly hear two beats
Our bodies intertwined underneath the sheets
I love you, and you constantly have some doubts
There's no need because you always have my whereabouts
I show you over and over again, there is no one like you
You reject me time after time; what's a girl to do
Look deep in the corners of my mind to find
What your heart needs, it belongs to mine
It's tough, and I'm willing to go that extra mile
And always be there to make your day a smile
You nodded at me on the first day we met
Too cute for words, and my number you did get
It's that smile, those lips, that little extra thing
That captured my heart and captured my dreams
Joy, you bring me joy, so much joy I have to tell it now
It wasn't easy, but you did, so please take a bow
Thinking of you now as you sleep in the next room
Even though you said you love me too, I assume
I'm wishing our bodies were intertwined as ever before
You do that thing you do, leaving me wanting more.

08/18/1995 Gerre' Flemons

My Worth

Closing my eyes and looking back over my years
Now I finally realize why I had so many tears
I loved you; you loved me; now we're done
My heart knew that you, you were not the one
Now I'm in my car trying to put words to a song
Exhaling trying to figure out exactly where I went wrong
With every beat, I move closer to the place
Where you used to hold my heart when it began to race
Trusting and loving till I can't feel love no more
Caressing me with your eyes because I was who you adored
My feet are on solid ground; I am back down to earth
You really didn't understand what I was really worth.

Proverb Woman

Have you ever noticed yourself watching him from afar
Underneath the moon, way beneath the stars
He takes your breath away with the love that knows only you
His heart melts every time you do that thing you do
You captivate, illuminate, make him weak in the knees
Because you are that Proverb woman and God is very pleased
Everything about you, from your head down to your toes
Shows him about how well you were made and his heart you do hold
The words that form out of your mouth, what you say
It's just a little bit of love and can go a very long way
What God has put together, let no man tear apart
You are the perfect man after God's own heart.

Touch of Me

Your heart, my heart tango as one
Today, tomorrow, our love has begun
I feel the warmth; I feel the beat
Touch of fire, touch of heat
Your body, my body, clasped so tight
Intertwined into the morning light
I feel free; I feel complete
Touch of you, touch of me
Gently we come, gently we cum
Voices in unison as we go numb
Limp bodies caress; limp bodies are wet
We just made the best sex yet
In the back of my mind, I see it... Oh so clear
Yet we make it a reality as we draw in near
Your body, my body, knows not when to quit
Like drugs, baby, we have to get that next hit
Ravishing me, ravishing you
We are on top of the world...just us two
Dynamite explodes; we explode like dynamite
I'll put you to bed, lights out, and goodnight.

08/12/2014 Gerre' Mua

Like You Say You Do

You are something special with a lot of wit and charm
You make me feel good each day when you touch me on the arm
You nibble on my ear and tell me that you really care
And look into my eyes and tell me that you will always be there
Deep down inside, I know you mean it like you say you do
On the outside, I don't show it, but baby, I truly love you
Remember what I say; it's the truth and not a lie
I will love you forever until the day I die.

11/07/1992 Gerre' Flemons

Remembering the Memories

I've always wanted to keep you in my possession
Without someone telling you or by hearing my confession
There's never been a love like you before
Each night I pray that you would come to my door
Take me away so no one would find you and me
And separate the both of us for time and all eternity
I never thought of the two of us being apart
I never imagined one day of you breaking my heart
It's all in the past, and now I'm ready to go
But memories of you continue to grow
In the back of my mind, I'll always think of you
And remember the things that we used to do.

10/13/1992 Gerre' Flemons

A Love Like Ours

A love like ours comes along once in a blue moon
I hope you never leave, and If you do, I hope it's not soon
A love like ours comes along once in a while
I hope by then we haven't lost our style
And If we ever part
Let's make a new start
Cause you're my dearest love
Straight sent from God above
Deep within, we have a power
Cause it's a love like ours.

11/17/1990 Gerre' Flemons

Leaving You

I've thought of leaving you once or twice
The thought came to me, and it wasn't very nice
That I could be leaving a man like you
The thought was dreadful and scary too
So I'm still thinking of a sure way
To tell you, baby, I'm gonna stay
Hearts are broken every day, and I won't break yours
You're the one I truly do adore
I rant, and I rave, but I can't get enough of your love
So no more of that, "I'm leaving you," not another shove
I want to grow old with you and be so good
Like all the other times that I knew that we would.

11/18/1990 Gerre' Flemons

Doing Things Together

I want to be there if you ever fall
Watch our kids go from scooting to a crawl
Walk with you in the lit-up park
Lay next to you in the deep, dark
Laugh when you tell a funny joke
Sip out of the same straw in your coke
Raise your children to be smart like you
These are just a few things we can do
If I must go on, I must say
Make love to you baby each and every day
Wash your back, and you wash mine
Drink a bottle of champagne or a glass of wine
Kiss you where you deserve to be kissed
Fulfill your dreams and conquer your wish
After all, I hope we'll be doing this forever
Because baby, I'll never leave you…never, never.
06/21/1994 Gerre' Flemons

11/18/1990 Gerre' Flemons

First Sight

When I first saw you, it was love at first sight
I wanted to get with you; I tried with all my might
I wrote a letter explaining who I was
Whenever I saw you, my stomach went "buzz"
Now we are together starting a new start
Let's not break up; I have a gentle heart
I like you, and I hope you like me
Let's make this relationship be all it can be.

08/27/1992 Gerre' Flemons

Coochie Drop

I really know how the coochie drop
I really know how the coochie pop
Eat it up, then slap and hit
Really know how to please this clit
Coochie drop all over you now
Coochie pop all over you now
Dripping like a running faucet
Tasty like sweet and sour sauces
Coochie dropping all in yo face
Coochie popping all over the place
Sexing it and loving it now
Fingering and sucking it now
Getting ready for the coochie drop
Getting ready for the coochie pop
Drop and pop all over you now
Catching everything that drops now
You're a man of many talents
Really strong so you can balance
All of this tasty coochie
And this big ol booty
Now that we're all done
And we've had some fun
Wipe off your big ol mouth
Cause you just came from the dirty south.

8/28/2019

August Mine

Chasing you in my dreams
Can't catch up with you
Wanting the lovemaking
That we used to do
Arms holding me so tight
Til I can't even breathe
It's amazing; your gentle touch
I don't want the feeling to leave
Push me down and collapse
Right on top of me
Gently rush in, and don't stop
Wait, I can't even breathe
Hold me and never let me go
For this can't ever end
I love the way this is going
From beginning to the end
Your face is fading fast
Your touch is ever light
This whole thing is fading
And I cannot see the light
Got to make this dream a reality
Cause I been missing you
Climb on top of me
And make it do what it do
I'm riding this time
And there are no brakes

August Mine (cont.)

Slow grinding and moving
And now I got the shakes
I hope you're caught up
And we're on the same page
Cause I'm really ready
For us to move to the next stage
Squeezing and pumping
Where I do that little thing
Where your eyes roll back
And I can hear you sing...
My name that is
How melodious to the ear
I can't wait to meet yo ass
For another round, my dear
Keep up the great work
Tap me on my ass
Raise your ass up
And put on the gas
It's time to let go
Right at the same time.

08/28/2019

Grind

I've waited for so long
For this very slow grind.
Slow grind leads to slow wind
That leads to lovemaking
You got that "ish" that makes it easy for my body aching
Taking it all in where you'll need to slow down
I need to match every bump and grind when I cum up to the mound
It's a long, thick, juicy piece of meat, and I need it now
Ima give it everything I got; I'm going pound for pound
Stand up in it and hang on really tight to my hips
I wanna give you all of me as you suck on my lips
Pleasure is the name of this lovemaking hook
When we're down with this thing, we call it "You Got Shook"
I'm down for another and another just to please you
Making sure you stay with me and you do everything you do
That arch in my back as you flipping me just right
Ought to tell you that you can hit it with all your might
She moves where you move and answers all your calls
Them guts say meow when you're hitting all them walls.

08/28/2019

I Know You Love When...

I can feel it in the pit of my stomach, and I wonder...
Can you go deeper?
Can you make us one?
I'm spread eagle for you, baby, and I ponder...
Is it the hottest?
When will you cum?
I know you love me when I bite my bottom lip
I know you love me when I sway my little hips
I know you love me when I twinkle my nose
I know you love me when I rub my cold toes
On your back and down your legs
When I rub your big ole head
Two bodies smacking to the rhythm of their own sexual beat
It's worth the climax, and I'm mimicking your stroke
Are we there yet?
Is it ours as one?
You flipped me over on my stomach, and I wonder...
Do you like this position?
When will you cum?
I know you love when I squeeze you so tight
I know you love when I hold you every night
I know you love when I give you all of me
I know you love when I see what you see
Through your eyes, it's crystal clear
Your love for me and how you hold me dear
Two bodies caressing and gelling to their own sensual heat
It's worth the climax,
and I'm mimicking your stroke
Are we there yet?

08/28/2019

Thank You

Dear Readers,

As we reach the end of this poetic journey together, I want to extend my heartfelt gratitude to each of you for taking the time to delve into the pages of this book. Your willingness to explore the tapestry of emotions, imagery, and reflections captured in these poems means the world to me. Poetry, at its core, is an intimate conversation between the writer and the reader, and I am honored that you have chosen to be part of this dialogue.

Thank you for allowing these words to resonate with you, and for bringing your own interpretations and experiences to them.

May the verses you've encountered here continue to inspire, comfort, and provoke thought long after you've turned the final page. With deepest appreciation and warmest wishes, I bid you farewell until our paths cross again in the world of words.

With gratitude,

Gerre' Myrte'

www.CollegeBoyPublishing.com
972-591-3739

www.ingramcontent.com/pod-product-compliance
Lightning Source LLC
Chambersburg PA
CBHW070103100426
42743CB00012B/2643